DIGITAL AND INFORMATION LITERACY ™

   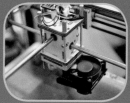

SMART MACHINES AND THE INTERNET OF THINGS

RYAN NAGELHOUT

rosen publishing's
rosen
central

New York

Published in 2016 by The Rosen Publishing Group, Inc.
29 East 21st Street, New York, NY 10010

Library of Congress Cataloging-in-Publication Data

Nagelhout, Ryan, author.
 Smart machines and the Internet of things / Ryan Nagelhout. — First Edition.
    pages cm. — (Digital and information literacy)
 Includes bibliographical references and index.
 ISBN 978-1-4994-3779-9 (library bound) — ISBN 978-1-4994-3777-5 (pbk.)
 — ISBN 978-1-4994-3778-2 (6-pack)
 1. Internet of things—Juvenile literature. I. Title.
 QA76.5915.N34 2015
 004.67'8–dc23
                                                            2015021316

Manufactured in the United States of America

CONTENTS

INTRODUCTION

Sometime in 2008, more things became connected to the Internet than there were people living on Earth. The "things" were more than just computers, phones, and tablets. The billions of different things were just about everything you can imagine. A Dutch company connected wireless sensors to cows that let farmers know when their cattle get sick or pregnant. People bought "smart" products like lightbulbs, connected televisions to the Internet to run apps, and programmed thermostats they controlled with their cell phones.

Former U.S. senator Ted Stevens once infamously described the Internet as a "series of tubes." The line became used as a kind of short-hand to describe the many people who struggle in understanding how the Internet actually works. However, these days Stevens's analogy isn't far from the truth. The Internet helps different things and people connect and communicate with one another through a series of wires, servers, and machines. This network is used by tiny bits of data to race around the world delivering messages, send files, and display information on computer screens.

Today's Internet, however, is used to connect many of the things people have never associated with computers until recently. For example, today's cell phones do much more than just make phone calls. They are

Managing the temperature and other settings inside the home has become much easier with tablet computers that are connected to smart technology.

"smart"; they are connected to the Internet and growing faster every year. More and more people than ever before read websites, make purchases, and send e-mails on their phones. Smartphones are essentially tiny computers that let individuals communicate in any number of ways, and it's just the start of this new technological revolution.

Vehicles are getting smarter and even faster with software updates pushed to them wirelessly. Electrical outlets can be turned off from anywhere in the world that has an Internet connection. A person can even track the amount of energy the plug is using and get updates pushed to a cell phone. Even watches and wearable devices are now connected to cell phones using simple technology that was once designed to link up computers. Wearable devices, for example, contain sensors and scanners that continuously monitor the individual user. Some wearable devices even have their own computer processing unit (CPU), hard drive, power supply, and input/output devices. They can communicate with the user and other wireless devices.

This interconnectivity of appliances, everyday objects, and people to the Web has been called by many different names. The "Internet of Everything" and "Industrial Internet" are two examples, but the most often used phrase is the "Internet of Things," or IoT. The term was coined by Kevin Ashton in 1999 during a meeting at a company called Proctor and Gamble (P & G). P & G wanted to improve the way it kept track of its products during production and shipping, but it soon realized that the ability to have connected sensors deliver information can be used in any number of ways.

Chapter 1

ARPANET to Internet

Computers were originally invented to do just that: compute. Numbers were input and they were crunched. Solutions were presented. But today's technology is used for much more than simple calculations. The Internet allows devices to interact with a wide variety of data produced by an infinite number of things. Today's Internet is much more than the server farms that connect laptops to desktops. The Internet of Things (IoT) is a complex structure that connects living, breathing creatures to the systems that make everyday life possible. Every day the world is becoming more connected. As machines begin to sense for themselves, these devices—and the people using them—are getting smarter along the way.

War Machines

This evolution of computer technology has happened fairly quickly. World War II, which lasted from 1939 to 1945, helped spark many of the earliest computing devices. Englishman Alan Turing built a machine to crack the

The Electronic Numerical Integrator and Computer was huge, measuring 1,800 square feet (167 square meters). It could add or subtract two ten-digit numbers at a speed of 5,000 per second.

German Enigma code system in 1939. Konrad Zuse's programmable Z3 was built for the Germans in 1941. What many consider to be the first true computer is the Electronic Numerical Integrator and Computer, or ENIAC. This machine was built in 1945, originally to help calculate the trajectory of shells during the war. The machine was finished after the war ended, but it was used by the U.S. Army for a decade. ENIAC even ran equations to help scientists research and build the hydrogen bomb during the Cold War.

The ENIAC was massive, a 1,800-square-foot (167-square-meter) machine full of vacuum tubes and diodes that worked together to create electrical circuits. These switches could be programmed with numbers and execute tasks. The 17,468 vacuum tubes helped the machine complete 5,000 instructions per second. By comparison, a smartphone today can complete 25 billion instructions per second. However, that kind of computing power was unheard of in 1945.

The initial concept of networked computers developed in the 1960s. In 1964, IBM began selling its System/360, a mainframe computer that connected to other, smaller machines called workstations. The mainframe held data and ran equations that connected workstations accessed and used for other tasks. These expensive machines (often costing about $2 million each) were also the first computers that could be upgraded. Different parts were replaced to make the machines work faster and last longer, which made businesses invest more in the technology.

WAN and Web

Computers got smaller, faster, and cheaper as time went on. The Apple 1 was released in 1976, and IBM's personal computer (PC) was released in 1981. They were also getting more connected thanks to the U.S. government. The Defense Advanced Research Projects Agency (DARPA) worked with researchers at the Massachusetts Institute of Technology (MIT) throughout the 1960s to create ARPANET. In 1965, the researchers connected the TX-2 computer in Massachusetts to the Q-32 in California using a dial-up phone connection, or phone line. It was the

File   Edit   View   Favorites   Tools   Help

THE INTERNET TOASTER

The Internet Toaster

Long before billions of modern things were connected to the Internet, there was a single toaster. The first Internet-connected device was a simple Sunbeam Deluxe toaster. In 1989, John Romkey was challenged on a radio show to connect a toaster to the Internet. It took a year of tinkering, but in 1990, Romkey and Simon Hackett debuted their "Internet Toaster" at the Interop Internet Networking Show.

The setup was simple: the two connected a computer to the toaster through Internet Protocol (IP). The power switch of the toaster was connected to the printer port of a network-connected laptop computer. Once it was connected, they used the protocol program to send commands to the toaster. Typing a command through the IP on a networked computer could turn the toaster on or off, or make toast pop up. The longer the toaster was on,

A toaster isn't the most practical appliance to connect to the Internet, but using Internet Protocol to toast bread showed what the technology could achieve with everyday objects.

the darker the toast would be. In 1991, Romkey and Hackett added a small robotic arm to the toaster. The arm was also connected to the Internet and could pick up a piece of bread, drop it into the toaster, and lift the toast out when it was finished.

It wasn't particularly efficient, but it changed how people thought the Internet could be used. At the time, only about 300,000 computers were online. The entire system was designed to move information back and forth. Connecting a toaster to the Internet was mostly a joke, and many jested that refrigerators and microwave ovens would soon be online as well. Although silly and not very practical, the Internet Toaster got people thinking. If they *could* connect appliances and other things to the Internet, what would they actually want to do with them?

first wide-area network, or a network made of computers spread across a wide geographical area.

The general concept of ARPANET was to create a secure system of communicating that wouldn't fail if a single connection was lost. ARPANET used something called packet switching, which took information and broke it down into small bits of data called packets. These packets could be sent to a single destination through a number of different routes. This operation meant that if one connection was broken, the packets could be collected by a single source and reassembled at the destination. This process also meant that the file could be sent faster. Decades later, packet switching and the partial transfer of data through packets are two of the basic ideas that power much of the Internet.

Over time, more and more machines became connected together. DARPA and its researchers created a standard way for machines to communicate with one another, called the Transmission Control Protocol/

Internet Protocol (TCP/IP). The first e-mail was sent between devices in 1971. Telnet, the first non-government packet switching network, was created in 1973. USENET, a mail and file transfer network created at Duke University and the University of North Carolina at Chapel Hill, was invented in 1979.

The modern Internet was a direct product of ARPANET, which was renamed "the Internet" in 1995. The web pages people associate with that Internet, however, came from the creation of the World Wide Web. In 1990, Tim Berners-Lee invented the World Wide Web when he created the HyperText Markup Language (HTML). He based HTML on hypertext, which he had been studying for quite a while. He hoped that HTML could

Tim Berners-Lee's invention of HyperText Markup Language and the World Wide Web changed the idea of the Internet from a place where data is shared to a place where users visit websites using a web browser.

serve as a common language that all computers could read utilizing browser software. Using HTML and the World Wide Web enabled programs called web browsers, such as Netscape or Microsoft Internet Explorer, to follow links and send a query to a server. These directions allowed users to view a website. At the time he invented the World Wide Web, Berners-Lee could hold the entire Web on his NeXT computer.

Today's Internet browsers, such as Mozilla's Firefox, Apple's Safari, or Google Chrome, still search the Word Wide Web using a version of Hypertext Transfer Protocol (HTTP) to display websites. The "www" before a site's uniform resource locator (URL) isn't needed anymore, but at the time it was a revolution in what the growing Internet could achieve. Internet users could view information from thousands—and soon millions and billions—of different websites from a monitor anywhere in the world. Information zipped across networks and servers, delivering packets at speeds thought impossible a few decades earlier. The modern Internet was officially born.

Chapter 2

Screens to Things

The Internet was first designed to get information from one screen to another no matter how much distance lay between them. Over the years, networks grew, millions of servers were added, and millions more users were connected across the world. Dial-up connections gave way to much faster broadband options such as cable modems, digital subscriber lines (DSL), and fiber optic lines. Over time these methods were made affordable for businesses and individuals to connect to the Internet in their homes.

Wireless Connections

There are even some ways to access the Internet without using wired connections. These methods take the packets of zeroes and ones that make up binary code, translate them into radio waves, and move them from one place to another over the air. Different types of radio waves are broadcast at different frequencies. An AM or FM radio signal, for example, has a very large amplitude and can be picked up many miles from its original

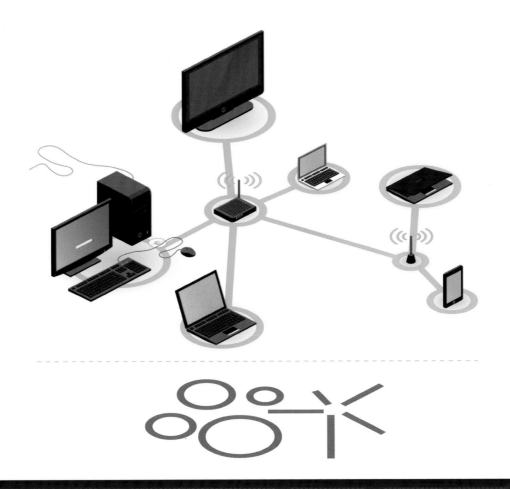

Computer networks are secure groups of connected devices—including laptops, phones, and tablets—that are connected to and make up the larger Internet.

broadcast point. The radio signals picked up by a car stereo are broadcast at a very low frequency. FM radio runs from 88 to 108 megahertz (MHz), which is a wave frequency containing millions of cycles per second. The radio waves used to access the Internet are broadcast at a much higher frequency. WiFi, for example, operates at a frequency of 2.4 or 5 gigahertz (GHz), which contains billions of cycles per second.

File   Edit   View   Favorites   Tools   Help

WHAT IS WIFI?

What Is WiFi?

WiFi stands for "wireless fidelity." It lets devices connect to the Internet by creating its own small over-the-air network using radio waves. These networks are called wireless local area networks (WLANs). A wireless transmitter, often called a wireless router, is connected directly to a high-speed Internet source. This router then broadcasts a network signal over a limited area. Devices that can use wireless next search for the signal, then negotiate a connection. Most networks are protected by a password to keep unwanted users out. The negotiation is complete when the network and device perform a "handshake." The device reads the WiFi signal, figures out its wavelength, and passes through any security measures it may have. When the handshake is complete, the device has Internet access.

There are a few problems with WiFi connections. For example, the range of a WiFi network is usually very small: only a few hundred feet (nearly 100 m). The signal strength of a WiFi network can also be affected by a number of things, such as concrete walls, tables, chairs, and even water. The signal of a WiFi network can also be impacted by microwaves, cordless phones, and other devices that use similar radio frequencies.

However, WiFi's lack of cabled Internet is essential to the IoT because it greatly expands what can be connected to the Internet. A single silicon computer chip carrying all the things necessary to connect something to the Internet can be added to all kinds of items. Small chips with similar Internet connectivity have existed for more than a decade, but the wide use of WiFi and the growth of 3G/4G technology have helped make the IoT become a reality.

Another way of connecting devices to the Internet is through cell phone technology. Unlike WiFi, which needs a local Internet source, 3G and 4G technology uses cell phone towers to connect to the Internet. The "G" stands for "generation," and each version number marks the rapid growth in connection speed of cell devices. As long as a tablet, cell phone, or other connected device is within range of a cell tower, 3G and 4G technology such as long-term evolution (LTE) can be used to move large amounts of information quickly.

Bluetooth

Bluetooth is another type of wireless communication that allows technology to connect and work together. Bluetooth devices connect, or pair, by searching for each other over very short distances. Bluetooth networks are often called personal area networks (PANs) and usually spread about 328 feet (100 m). Bluetooth devices have a small chip inside them that sends out and finds Bluetooth radio waves, then pairs with other Bluetooth-enabled devices to communicate.

Bluetooth can share a variety of information between enabled devices: music, data, voice, photos, and even videos. A computer may use Bluetooth to connect to a wireless mouse and keyboard, and a phone can connect to a Bluetooth-enabled car to play music or safely take phone calls while driving. Bluetooth can be used by smart devices to easily—and cheaply—connect to things that control them. Bluetooth technology was first invented in

Bluetooth can send music to another device or connect a speaker and audio receiver wirelessly to a cell phone to allow hands-free access to phone calls.

1994, but newer developments make the technology work more efficiently and use less power to operate, an important factor for battery-powered devices such as mobile phones, tablets, and laptops.

These wireless radio transmissions—WiFi, 3G/4G, and Bluetooth—are essential to the growth of the Internet of Things. Although WiFi and mobile data connections were first used to connect devices with screens—tablets, cell phones, and laptops—this technology had allowed other things in more remote locations to attach to computer networks. People soon realized that this connectivity could be used for more than just sharing information from one monitor or liquid crystal display (LCD) to another. Researchers, businesses, and even ordinary people began to question just what the Internet could be used for. After all, the more things they could connect to the Internet, the more data they would have to share.

This transition from screens to things is still fairly new, but with the technology now in place to make it possible, the growth has happened quickly. As the prices for smart devices continue to fall and more people experiment with smart technology in their homes and businesses, the industry continues to grow. Analytical firm Gartner says by 2020 there will be more than 26 billion connected devices spread all over the world. Some other firms say that number is too small, guessing the total will top 100 billion. Much like the toaster that started it all, if a device has an on-and-off switch, all it needs is a silicon chip to join the Internet of Things.

MYTHS & FACTS

MYTH The U.S. government controls the Internet.

FACT No one person or group controls the Internet. It is made up of a variety of networks controlled by different groups, people, and governments. Each has a certain level of control and access, but no one power controls the entire thing.

MYTH The Internet and the World Wide Web are the same thing.

FACT The Internet is much older than the World Wide Web. The Internet uses the TCP/IP to connect and send information between devices. The World Wide Web allows web browsers to display sites using HTTP and other protocols. The World Wide Web uses the Internet to communicate.

MYTH Bluetooth is an acronym, like WiFi, LTE, and TCP/IP.

FACT Bluetooth is actually named after Danish king Halard Blåtland, a Viking whose last name translates to "blue tooth." The Swedish company Ericsson used the name to honor Blåtland for his ability to bring people together.

Chapter 3

The Smart Home

One of the easiest-to-understand uses of the Internet of Things is the type of connections happening in the home. Internet-connected "things" in houses and apartments can be controlled from phones and other devices even when they are thousands of miles away. Those in a home that has a WiFi network can add smart things to that network and use them as they see fit. But just because it's possible, why do people want smart devices? The answers are not always the same for everyone. Some use them to save money by making their homes more energy efficient. Others want added security or to use their entertainment systems more effectively.

More advanced smart technology includes a bed from Luna that monitors your health and sleep phases and can talk to other smart devices such as lights. Smart appliances such as slow cookers, coffee makers, and heaters can be remotely accessed for cooking and many other uses. Each smart home is different because it is highly customizable. Users can choose which smart items they need and adjust some settings, usually with

A smart oven could be used remotely to start dinner with a cell phone connection before a homeowner returns from work, saving him or her time and making it easier to cook on busy days.

the help of a smartphone or tablet, to make them work together. In this way, a smart home is whatever a user wants it to be.

Saving Energy

Reducing energy usage is good for two big reasons: it saves people money on their heating and electric bills, and it means less energy needs to be created at power plants that use fossil fuel sources such as oil, coal, and natural gas. In that way, using less energy is good for the environment! There are many different smart devices that can help reduce energy use in the home.

Until recently, lightbulbs had not changed much since their invention in the late 1800s. Inside the round glass tube is gas and a fragile light source called a filament, which gets very hot and burns out quickly. Over the last few decades, newer technology has all but replaced those simple devices. Newer bulbs, called compact fluorescent lamps (CFLs), waste less energy and last much longer than traditional bulbs.

Another kind of lightbulb, called a light emitting diode (LED), is used in a true smart bulb. LEDs are made of tiny electronic circuits that create light when powered by electricity. These circuits are grouped together and make

LED lightbulbs, such as the Philips HUE personal wireless lights, can be used to display different colors and brightness levels and save energy in a smart home system.

a very bright light that lasts for years, much longer than traditional bulbs. LEDs can also change color! LEDs can come in many different colors, such as red or green. Some LED smart bulbs can even change into hundreds of colors. Philips, for example, has a smart lightbulb called the HUE that comes with a base that helps control each lightbulb throughout a home. A homeowner connects his or her smartphone to the base using an application, or app, then changes the color and brightness of up to fifty different bulbs at a time. The app even lets users import a photo and pick out colors in it, which the bulb can mimic. HUE bulbs can also be timed to do different things throughout the day, helping people wake up in the morning with bright lights or change colors when the sun begins to set in the evening.

The Hub

Many different companies make similar WiFi-enabled smart bulbs. To work properly, they need to connect to a hub, a networking device that allows them to communicate with both a home's WiFi network and the apps needed to configure the devices. These hubs—such as the one in Belkin's WeMo system—work together with other smart things like smart power outlets or light switches. These devices can be used to turn power on and off at certain times of the day, or even remotely from a smartphone. This ability is useful in a number of ways. If someone forgot to turn a light off before that person left for vacation, he or she could take out the mobile device and flip the switch by using the app, no matter where that individual is located.

Remotely switching power outlets and lights on and off is much like the "Internet Toaster" that started the IoT all those years ago. Any "dumb" appliance or device can be turned on and off from any location. Slow cookers in the kitchen can be turned on to start making dinner well before someone gets home. A video game console can be turned off after an update is completed. Anything that needs power to operate can be managed by a single tap on a smartphone.

Thermostats and Batteries

Another area where people can save money is with their home's heating and cooling. A WiFi-enabled thermostat, such as a Nest, can be controlled with a smartphone and can change temperatures in the home quickly. The Nest thermostat learns the habits of the people living in the house and can make its own programs, setting temperatures lower or higher when people are in or outside of the home. This capability saves money and offers a level of customization a basic thermostat can't provide.

Further energy savings can come from a more direct source: home-owners installing their own power sources, such as solar panels, which take in sunlight and generate energy. Some solar panel setups are simple and power the filter of a swimming pool or a light in a shed. However, some are used directly with the principal power source of a home, which is connected to the main energy grid. In 2015, the electric car company Tesla began selling a battery—called the PowerWall—that can be installed in a home. This battery stores energy from solar panels but also allows homeowners to purchase energy at off-peak hours—when it is much less expensive—from the traditional electrical grid.

Tesla's PowerWall system, seen here at its unveiling, lets homeowners save money by collecting energy for their homes with a battery pack they keep inside the home.

File   Edit   View   Favorites   Tools   Help

IF THIS THEN THAT

If This Then That

If This Then That, or IFTTT, is a Web-based service that started in 2010. The service allows users to make their own "recipes," or triggers, for certain actions to happen at particular times. The recipes are simple: if a certain condition is met, the recipe makes sure another thing also happens. For example, one recipe says that if a photo is uploaded to the Web service Instagram, it will then automatically save a copy of it with the file-sharing program Dropbox.

There are an endless amount of recipes to make using a variety of different platforms. Some recipes are based on sending e-mails or reminders, while others use smart technology to automate certain tasks. People set recipes to send e-mails to others, send reminders to themselves, or even arrange a fake phone call if they need an excuse to leave a dinner table! More complex recipes can turn on smart lights when a smartphone's GPS location gets close to its home, or turn up a home's smart thermostat when the temperature outside drops below a certain degree.

Users borrow recipes made by others or model their own on them to customize the experience however they want. IFTTT has evolved to use smart technology directly, such as the HUE lightbulb, but many IFTTT creators have used the service to interact with millions of different smart things. IFTTT is a simple way to look at computer programming because very little language is required to make it work. Recipes can be created on the fly through a smartphone app following simple instructions, linking devices and services together to work smarter and more efficiently. In 2015, the app split between IF recipes and DO recipes, which are simple one-button commands that work directly with certain devices. As more devices become smart, If This Then That becomes a more useful tool for people experimenting with smart things.

Entertainment

Internet-connected televisions are some of the most popular smart things. Smart TVs have their own apps and can stream music, movies, and run other programs when attached to a WiFi network or a wired connection. Many DVD players, sound systems, and video game systems are also Internet-connected and have similar apps. Many people make their own entertainment systems using small computers, with their televisions acting as monitors and adding Bluetooth keyboards to use the computer as a media center. One tiny computer, called Raspberry Pi, is very popular with people who like to custom-build computers to complete different tasks. Raspberry Pi kits can be used for any number of different things, including playing old video games, working as a spy camera, or even building a weather station.

Security Systems

Many homes have security systems, but new technology allows these systems to do things homeowners never thought possible. Through the use of a smartphone app, homeowners can check WiFi-enabled cameras, such as a Dropcam, inside their house or apartment. These cameras record video but can also be looked at in real time to check in on pets or look for other problems while they are away. Some of these systems, such as door and window sensors, work together with other smart security devices in the home. There are smart locks that, along with keys, can be locked and unlocked through a smartphone app. Even garage door openers have WiFi connections that allow users to open and close their garages remotely.

At the very least, smart locks and other security devices help forgetful people keep their belongings safe. HTC even has a device called the Fetch, which is attached to a set of keys. Fetch connects to a smartphone and will beep if people leave their phone or keys behind somewhere. It also maps their last location through a global positioning system (GPS), which helps people locate these items if they become lost.

TEN GREAT QUESTIONS
TO ASK A CYBER SECURITY EXPERT

1   How secure is my WiFi network?

2   Can other people access my smart devices?

3   Can hackers access my smart network?

4   Who can access my network's data?

5   Will my doors open when the power goes out on my smart locks?

6   Does my data go to a server somewhere?

7   What if my phone or laptop gets stolen? Can my smart devices be accessed?

8   What do companies do with my smart network information?

9   How often should I change my passwords?

10   Should I trust companies making smart products to keep my information safe?

Chapter 4

The Smart World

The Internet of Things is a revolution in the home, but many of the things that now interact with the Internet work outside of a WiFi network. These things need a dedicated connection to a 3G or 4G network, or they need to use services such as GPS to track locations in real time.

These connections allow data to be automatically added to the IoT and used in a variety of ways. Adding smart things to the world means that information is no longer simply moved from screen to screen. These billions of things add data to global networks instantly and can be accessed for an endless array of purposes, many of which are automated by other things themselves. For example, the temperature outside is not manually typed into a computer; it is measured by a sensor somewhere and its data is sent around the world, triggering e-mail reminders to a person to wear a jacket or bring an umbrella if rain is in the forecast. The screens may still be the destination for much of this information, but the data no longer needs to be inputted by hand. Real-time uses for the IoT can be as simple as someone using a phone that has GPS to confirm that a person will be late for a meeting, then automatically sending other attendees an e-mail or text message to let them know about the delay. Smart devices and programs can be used in an ever-growing variety of fields.

City Living

Using data from sensors at water treatment facilities, facility managers can control cities' water supplies to help fight rising prices during droughts. Cities themselves are becoming smarter. In Helsinki, Finland, sensors on the city's buses have helped drivers cut down on fuel usage and make rides smoother and safer. Classrooms in China and the United States are becoming smarter, using digital whiteboards and tablets to

IoT technology is being used in classrooms. A teacher shows information about students' hearts on an interactive digital whiteboard, also called a smartboard.

help students learn. Even public safety has been improved: an intelligent 9-1-1 response system has helped police, fire, and emergency crews work together to solve problems more quickly than ever before.

Health Care

Data collected by smart devices can even help doctors monitor patients inside and outside of hospitals and better diagnose problems that the patients may have. That data can be shared more efficiently, helping improve health care around the world. Wearing sensors that track biometrics or track fitness activities like running or walking help people stay healthy and out of the doctor's office.

Smart Vehicles

Today's cars have many parts that contain computers. Even the simplest new car on the market has at least thirty tiny computers inside managing everything from the spark plugs to the locks on the doors. As cars fill with more electronics and computer technology, they've been added to the IoT in a variety of ways. Many cars are connecting to cell networks and broadcast a WiFi network to which passengers can connect their devices.

Tesla's vehicles, which are all electric, can even

Smart medical technology may not be the default option for most doctors, but it could be the difference between life and death in emergency care.

File   Edit   View   Favorites   Tools   Help

    THE IOT AND SAFETY

The IoT and Safety

Many smart devices are meant to make homes and businesses safer, but there are concerns about the safety of these devices. Billions of network-connected devices mean billions of opportunities for hackers to gain access to networks and the information stored on them. In 2013, computer hackers accessed Target's secure network through the heating and cooling systems used in its stores by using malware installed on its registers. The hackers stole credit card information from millions of people.

Many critics of the Internet of Things say WiFi devices are very easy targets for those trying to gain network access. In 2015, DefCon, the largest hacker convention in the United States, hosted an "Internet of Things Village" that allowed hackers to build—and break into—Internet-connected things such as routers, refrigerators, smart cars, and smart home technology. Many hackers work to help technology makers find weak spots in security technology, but many worry that easy access to devices and networks for hackers will lead to more security failures in the future.

Others worry about giving machines too much control over individuals' lives. Self-driving cars or airplanes have many worried about what happens when those machines break down or fail. Relying too much on technology to complete basic tasks may be harmful if these devices are hacked, or even if they just stop working. People need to trust smart technology for it to be used, and businesses are spending lots of time and money ensuring that these devices are safe and secure.

download updates to make the cars more fuel efficient or fix other problems with their software. Smart cars have entire systems dedicated to sending text messages, answering calls, and playing music, allowing drivers hands-free access to the technology while the cars are in motion. Many companies are hoping to take people out of the driver's seat altogether. Google is working on self-driving car technology that uses GPS to navigate and sensors on the car to avoid crashing into obstacles. Uber, an app-based taxi service, also hopes to use driverless cars in the future.

Google's self-driving cars are being tested right now, and the company hopes that they will one day take humans out of the driver seat of all vehicles on the road.

Animals and Research

It's not just humans that can benefit from the Internet of Things. Scientists are attaching tracking devices to endangered animals and learning more about them as they travel all around the world, even in places too remote or dangerous for people to visit. These data points are helping scientists save threatened animal populations by learning more about how they live and reproduce, and how human actions are interfering with their habitats.

The IoT can even assist people's pets. Sensors on a dog or cat collar can help find lost pets miles away from home. The GPS company Garmin even has tools for training and tracking dogs that work with hunters. Tagg's pet tracker can alert users when the temperature around a dog gets dangerously hot or cold, or if the animal's health or behavior shows any sign of injury.

Chapter 5

The Future of Things

In the 1999 made-for-TV movie *Smart House*, a widower and his two children win a contest and move into a fully automated home full of high-tech gadgets. At first the house seems too good to be true. The technology—a home that cooks and cleans on its own—was impossible to imagine at the time. Of course, in the movie, the home's artificial intelligence soon goes haywire. The teen son tinkers with the computer, named PAT, and it starts to act like an overly protective mother, finally taking the family hostage inside the home.

More than a decade later, the *Smart House* concept still sounds impossible to imagine. Entire homes having the same artificial intelligence is a futuristic dream similar to that found in some science fiction movies. However, the fully automated home has gotten much closer to becoming reality in recent years. More and more devices can be connected to work in tandem. People can play with If This Then That to create recipes that automate many Internet-based tasks. Tinkering doesn't create an artificial intelligence disaster like in the *Smart House* movie; however, it can make life considerably easier.

Many people hope the growth of smart technology will make living easier by connecting their favorite things together into one easy-to-use system of gadgets. Here, a home's power generation and use can be viewed on a TV screen.

Many different companies have invested an enormous amount of time and money in developing the technology for the IoT. This backing means that as supply of these devices grows, the cost of buying and using these things will go down. Companies making money off the Internet of Things will continue to develop more products that they think people will use.

File   Edit   View   Favorites   Tools   Help

E-JUNK AND THE IOT

E-Junk and the IoT

One of the biggest problems with the speed of technology growth is the waste it leaves behind. As devices get faster and cheaper, older ones become obsolete and need replacing. Many of these devices—tube monitors, old hard drives, and other computer parts—are made of metals that are rare or even toxic. They can be dangerous to throw out and do not decompose quickly.

E-waste, or e-junk, is a growing problem around the world. In 2013, United Nations University estimated that nearly 73,854,858 tons (about 67,000,000 metric tons) of electronics and equipment hit the computer market, while 58,422,500 tons (53 million metric tons) of e-waste was thrown out worldwide. As more and more devices become smart, those numbers are only expected to grow. E-junk is only 2 percent of the trash in U.S. landfills,

As e-waste piles up, many people worry that they are going through devices too quickly. Advances in technology cause them to replace devices before they actually stop working.

but it represents 70 percent of its toxic waste. The Stopping the E-waste Problem (StEP) initiative predicts that by 2017 the total annual volume of e-waste will rise to 65.4 million per year, a 33 percent raise. As people buy new cell phones every two years and upgrade their homes with smart devices, more and more e-waste is thrown away and little has been done to address e-waste recycling.

However, some smart technology has been developed to help keep devices from becoming obsolete. This installation of new or modified parts to something already built is called retrofitting. For example, in 2015 Asus and Google released the Chromebit, a computer small enough to be plugged into a television or monitor. The Chromebit is similar to Google's Chromecast, which was released in 2013. Chromecast creates a secure subnet of a wireless network that allows connected smart devices to stream media such as television shows and movies to screens that do not have smart capabilities. These tiny "smart" devices could add usefulness to so-called "dumb" televisions and moni-tors for years to come, limiting the growing technology waste that the planet Earth faces.

One device that appears to make good on that promise is Amazon Dash, a WiFi connected button that, when pushed, automatically orders a product such as laundry detergent. Amazon Dash saves Amazon customers a trip to the store or even a trip to their computers. Amazon hopes that the products people use often and run out of—paper towels, bottles of water, and even macaroni and cheese—will be reordered on its site at the press of a button.

One of the unique aspects about the smart things industry is that nothing about the IoT is essential. No one really needs a WiFi-connected

A smart coffee machine could save someone time in the morning or even have a hot cup of coffee ready for them when they come home from a long day at work.

lock for a door or a lightbulb that can change from green to blue when a person is half a world away. These things could fulfill a purpose—lock a door and light up a room—without an Internet connection. However, as the Internet of Things continues to grow, it becomes more and more helpful. The invention of the Internet has changed the way many live their lives. Lots of people feel that—just like cars, computers, and the other technology people now take for granted—it's only a matter of time before smart things become as essential to individuals' daily lives as the Internet is now.

GLOSSARY

artificial intelligence The idea and creation of computer systems that can perform jobs that usually humans are needed to do, such as speaking, decision making, and visual tasks.

automatically Done without thought or intention.

biometrics Measurements that track the human body and its health.

Bluetooth A wireless technology standard for exchanging data over short distances via radio frequencies.

customize To build, fit, or change to suit a specific person.

efficient Doing something in a way that doesn't produce waste.

fidelity The degree to which an electronic device can reproduce something.

fragile Easily broken, delicate.

hypertext A computer system that lets users move to new information by clicking on highlighted text.

malware Any mischievous, harmful, or intrusive type of software, including viruses, worms, spyware, and other programs.

negotiate To have a discussion with another so as to arrive at an agreement.

obsolete Out of date.

protocol A set of rules for the formatting of data in an electronic communications system.

query A question or request for information about something.

subnet A subdivision of an IP network.

trajectory The curved angle or path along which something travels.

WiFi Technology that allows an electronic device to exchange data or connect to the Internet wirelessly using radio waves.

FOR MORE INFORMATION

Canadian Internet Registration Authority (CIRA)
350 Sparks Street, Suite 306
Ottawa, ON K1R 7S8
Canada
(613) 237-5335
Website: http://cira.ca/
CIRA regulates all .ca domain name services, the standard domain of
    Canada. It promotes secure and equal access to the Internet for all
    Canadians.

Canadian Radio-television and Telecommunications Commission
Ottawa, ON K1A 0N2
Canada
(877) 249-2782
Website: http://www.crtc.gc.ca/
The Canadian Radio-television and Telecommunications Commission
    handles Internet policies and regulation in Canada.

Computer History Museum
1401 North Shoreline Boulevard
Mountain View, CA 94043
(650) 810-1010
Website: http://www.computerhistory.org
The mission of the Computer History Museum is to preserve and present
    for posterity the artifacts and stories of the information age. The
    website includes online exhibits about inventions, applications, and
    the people who were behind the inventions. It also provides a time-
    line and information about educational programs for young people.

Defense Advanced Research Projects Agency (DARPA)
675 North Randolph Street
Arlington, VA 22203-2114
(703) 526-6630
Website: http://www.darpa.mil/
DARPA is a leading research organization and part of the United States
    military. It works with researchers who study technology to aid in
    national security and other projects.

Federal Communications Commission
445 12th Street SW
Washington, DC 20554
(888) 225-5322
Website: http://www.fcc.gov/
The Federal Communications Commission monitors communication
    through radio, television, wire, satellite, and cable. It handles com-
    plaints from consumers and sets standards for communications
    technology in the United States.

Federal Trade Commission (FTC)
600 Pennsylvania Avenue
Washington, DC 20580
(202) 326-2222
Website: https://www.ftc.gov/
The FTC protects consumers and answers complaints they may have about a
    variety of industries, including technology such as computers and other
    smart technologies. Its Bureau of Consumer Protection safeguards
    people from unfair or deceptive business practices.

Institute of Electrical and Electronics Engineers (IEEE)
3 Park Avenue, 17th Floor
New York, NY 10016-5997
(800) 678-4333
Website: https://www.ieee.org/
The IEEE is the largest professional association for the advancement of
   technology in the world. It helps make standards and other deci-
   sions for Internet-based technology.

World Wide Web Foundation
1110 Vermont Avenue NW, Suite 500
Washington, DC 20005
(202) 595-2892
Website: http://webfoundation.org/
The World Wide Web Foundation helps people all over the world connect to the Internet affordably and intends to keep it decentralized,
   open, and free for all people.

Websites

Because of the changing nature of Internet links, Rosen Publishing has
developed an online list of websites related to the subject of this book.
This site is updated regularly. Please use this link to access the list:

http://www.rosenlinks.com/DIL/Smart

FOR FURTHER READING

Bily, Cynthia A. *The Internet*. Farmington Hills, MI: Greenhaven Press, 2012.

Bodden, Valerie. *Internet*. Mankato, MN: Creative Education, 2008.

Chmielewski, Gary T. *How Did That Get to My House?* Internet. North Mankato, MN: Cherry Lake Publishing, 2009.

Gerber, Larry. *Cloud-based Computing* (Digital Information and Literacy). New York, NY: Rosen Publishing, 2012.

Greengard, Samuel. *The Internet of Things*. Cambridge, MA: MIT Press, 2015.

Hollander, Barbara Gottfried. *The Next Big Thing: Developing Your Digital Business Idea*. New York, NY: Rosen Publishing, 2012.

Kellmereit, Daniel, and Daniel Obodovski. *The Silent Intelligence: The Internet of Things*. San Francisco, CA: DnD Ventures, 2013.

McEwen, Adrian, and Hakim Cassimally. *Designing the Internet of Things*. Hoboken, NJ: Wiley, 2013.

Pfister, Cuno. *Getting Started with the Internet of Things: Connecting Sensors and Microcontrollers to the Cloud*. Sebastopol, CA: O'Reilly Media, 2011.

Swanson, Jennifer, and Glen Mullay. *How the Internet Works*. Mankato, MN: Child's World, 2012.

Weber, Rolf H., and Romana Weber. *Internet of Things: Legal Perspectives*. Berlin, Germany: Schulthess, 2010.

Willard, Nancy E. *Cyber-Safe Kids, Cyber-Savvy Teens: Helping Young People Learn to Use the Internet Safely and Responsibly*. San Francisco, CA: Jossey-Bass, 2007.

Woodford, Chris. *Digital Technology*. New York, NY: Chelsea House, 2006.

BIBLIOGRAPHY

Brandon, John. "How Does a Wi-Fi Signal Work?" Retrieved May 11, 2015 (http://mentalfloss.com/article/57916/how-does-wi-fi-signal-work).

Cisco. "Internet of Things (IoT)." Retrieved May 11, 2015 (http://www.cisco.com/web/solutions/trends/iot/overview.html).

Computer History Museum. "Computer History Timeline." Retrieved May 11, 2015 (http://www.computerhistory.org/timeline/?category=cmptr).

Dashevsky, Evan. "A Remembrance and Defense of Ted Stevens' 'Series of Tubes.'" PC Magazine, June 5, 2014. Retrieved May 19, 2015 (http://www.pcmag.com/article2/0,2817,2458760,00.asp).

Dutton, Gail. "Home Security 2015: The Internet of Things (IoT) Brings Innovation AND Danger." Retrieved May 11, 2015 (http://www.forbes.com/sites/sungardas/2015/04/08/home-security-2015-the-internet-of-things-iot-brings-innovation-and-danger/).

Gibbs, Samuel. "Amazon Moves Towards 'Internet of Things' Shopping with Dash." Retrieved May 11, 2015 (http://www.theguardian.com/technology/2015/apr/01/amazon-dash-button-internet-of-things).

Gibbs, Samuel. "Samsung Pledges Over $100m to Make an Open 'Internet of Things' Finally Happen." Retrieved May 11, 2015 (http://www.theguardian.com/technology/2015/jan/06/samsung-pledges-over-100bn-to-make-an-open-internet-of-things-finally-happen).

Goldman, Russell. "How Did Hackers Breach Target's Security Net?" Retrieved May 11, 2015 (http://abcnews.go.com/blogs/headlines/2013/12/how-did-hackers-breach-targets-security-net/).

Greenough, John. "Security Will Be Critical to the Success or Failure of Internet of Things Products." Retrieved May 11, 2015 (http://www.businessinsider.com/ftc-top-recommendations-for-protecting-home-iot-2015-3).

Morgan, Jacob. "A Simple Explanation of 'The Internet of Things.'"
   Retrieved May 11, 2015 (http://www.forbes.com/sites/jacobmor-
   gan/2014/05/13/simple-explanation-internet-things-that-anyone-
   can-understand/).
Newton, Thomas. "Internet Connected Toasters: A History." Retrieved
   May 11, 2015 (https://recombu.com/digital/article/internet-
   connected-toasters-a-history_M10281.html).
Wasik, Bill. "In the Programmable World, All Our Objects Will Act as
   One." Retrieved May 11, 2015 (http://www.wired.com/2013/05/
   internet-of-things-2/all/).
Wortham, Jenna. "A Web Tool That Lets You Automate the Internet."
   Retrieved May 11, 2015 (http://bits.blogs.nytimes.com/
   2011/09/23/a-web-tool-that-lets-you-automate-the-internet/).

INDEX

About the Author

Ryan Nagelhout has written several nonfiction works for young people, including books on drones, military helicopters, early computers, cars, and early cameras. He is also a journalist who lives in Niagara Falls, New York. He has a B.A. degree in communication studies with a concentration in journalism from Canisius College in Buffalo, New York. A former newspaper reporter in Niagara Falls, he uses the Internet to podcast with a friend in Virginia and eagerly awaits the day when he can install a smart thermostat in his home.

Photo Credits

Cover, p. 1 (inset, left to right) Canadapanda/Shutterstockcom, moodboard/Thinkstock, Peshkova/iStock/Thinkstock, palickam/iStock/Thinkstock; p. 5 BrianAJackson/iStock/Thinkstock; p. 8 Francis Miller/The LIFE Picture Collection/Getty Images; pp. 10, 22, 32, 35 Bloomberg/Getty Images; p. 12 Science and Society/SuperStock; p. 15 © iStockphoto.com/Anil Yanik; p. 17 fantom_rd/Shutterstock.com; p. 21 Ethan Miller/Getty Images; p. 24 Kevork Djansezian/Getty Images; p. 29 © iStockphoto.com/davidf; p. 30 Yoshikazu Tsuno/AFP/Getty Images; p. 36 Zoran Milich/Moment Mobile/Getty Images; p. 38 © iStockphoto.com/Chesky W; cover and interior pages (pixels) © iStockphoto.com/suprun

Designer: Nicole Russo; Editor: Kathy Kuhtz Campbell; Photo Researcher: Bruce Donnola